T0128236

The Heart of Poetry

THROUGH DARK INK TO LIGHT PAPER

Jessica L Shahinian

authorHOUSE®

AuthorHouse™
1663 Liberty Drive
Bloomington, IN 47403
www.authorhouse.com
Phone: 1 (800) 839-8640

Published by AuthorHouse   02/08/2016

ISBN: 978-1-5049-6375-6 (sc)
ISBN: 978-1-5049-6376-3 (e)

Print information available on the last page.

Any people depicted in stock imagery provided by Thinkstock are models, and such images are being used for illustrative purposes only. Certain stock imagery © Thinkstock.

Th is book is printed on acid-free paper.

Table of Contents

I'm dedicating my book to one of the few who I told about my past and held me while I cried. He then said "Let's go get drunk and make-out". He was my best friend who became lost at the bottom of a glass due to insecurities and depression. His death was unexpected and a devastating blow to my life. I will forever love you Dan Cannon.

Note to Readers:

"Please be warned": If you struggle with depression, much like I did, where nothing in the world could make you happy, this book may seem to initially encourage you to listen to those ideas of suicide, murder and all attempts of killing mankind but please note there are additional pages to this book that will hopefully transition you through that and into something better. Find an escape like I did [poetry] and make it your bitch. Keep in mind that most known works of art, poetry and novels are dark, demented and completely insane; the artists always come out alive (until their imminent and usually natural death, of course). If you can't find the significance in my work and my intentions on publishing it, please continue to take your meds; you'll get there soon.

THE SURRENDERING HEART

Loneliness

Alone
What a word to say
Makes you want to groan
It turns you gray
It has no meaning
I don't think about it much
Feelings
Something you can't touch
It means no one
Not anybody
Not someone
Not a somebody
Crouching in a corner
You cry all night
No one cares
There is no light

1995

Love Forever

Here I lay in my room
Sobbing with no control
Staring at his picture
Sinking into my own sorrow

I don't truly understand
Why I hurt so terribly much
I've never felt such pain
Like my heart is in his hand, crushed

Why won't it just go away
And leave me to my sorrow
Maybe it's temporary lust
And yet, I know, I'll feel it tomorrow

I always suffer through this
When I see or think of him
As if caught in the middle of an ocean
With no knowledge of how to swim.

1995

My Pain

I wallow in my pain
And sink in my sorrow
Desperately hoping
For no tomorrow.
How would the world
React to my pain?
Could explain my horror
What would they gain?
No such thing as love
I have come to conclude
Not even parental love
All mean and cruel
Was I brought here
To be tortured and slain?
Finally the day has come
Where I feel nothing but pain.
Now I long for death
There is nothing to live for
I hear the constant lies
I don't want to hear anymore.

1996

No Emotions

I want to crawl inside your body
Diseasing everything that makes you function
Taking anything into custody
Building your mutation
I want to tear your insides out
To see what color you are
I'll show you what pain's all about
And paint you with alcohol and tar
I want to strip you clean of emotions
So no crying is allowed
With creativity there are creations
I'm sure mom would be proud
My feelings don't matter
But through my pain and crying
I wanted you to know
Because of you, I'm dying

1997

The End

Waiting around
Thinking of something
Slowly dissolving
Turning to nothing

Hoping for love
To just pop up
Lost in a fantasy
The size of a cup

The ground starts to rock
Grabs onto a soul
The world is spinning
And swallows it whole

Earth slowly stops
Life is vanished
The living is lost
The earth has diminished

1997

99 Ways to Die

Crashing in a car
Pushed off a train
Stabbed with a knife
Drowned in the rain
Shot with a gun
Over dosed on pills
So many murders
So many kills
Bleed to death
Lack of oxygen
Beat to death
By several men
You've had a great life
Yes, you've had lots of fun
99 ways to die
Now choose one

2000

Death

Slowly waking up
Trying to stall
Look to the sky
And see bodies fall
Hoping it's a dream
Only to be disappointed
Licking up the blood
Where the bodies have connected
Now wondering where
The bodies came from
See the grim reaper
Know your time has come
Death is coming
You can smell it near
Soon you realize
Death is here

2002

One Thought

I step up to the ledge
The wind is so strong
Feels as though I'm being encouraged
To jump and end my disaster

Love
It's a crazy thing to feel
Are you feeling it?
Or is it that you want to feel it?

Trust
People get confused easily
Most feel jealousy and envy
'It's not that I don't trust you...'

Bullshit!
You don't trust me to say no?
To hold my grounds for our love?
Your lack of 'trust' hurts me deeply

Loyalty
I was so loyal
But accused of infidelity almost constantly
Still I kept my promise to be true to you

(continued)

Testing
Always testing my patience
My commitment to you was never enough
Always doing wrong in your eyes

Compromising
God…it was never ending
Coming to a point where I no longer could
Changing ourselves completely was never the plan

My toes hang off the edge
Funny how thick the air feels
Heart's racing, but my mind is finally clear
As I let go, all I think is "I'll always love you"

2007

Debilitated

The pain may subside
Or I scream all day
Tear apart my patience
Tears of frustration as I lay

The doctors will keep prescribing
And tearing down my soul
One defect after defect
Until I am no longer whole

People still will criticize
Neglecting all my pain
Never feeling quite alive
Never able to quite explain

The wearing down through the years
Will ultimately end my agony
When finally I can lay down
And welcome my tragedy

2006

THE BROKEN HEART

Men

First things first
They say they lost their keys
When they want you to lose more than that
In their back seat
Commitment
True devotions
Vocabulary not known
They have no definition
They're the masters of deception
Corruption
Evil
Perversion
Just one common thing
I can't help mention
Muting us out
In their soundproof dimension

1996

Confused

I've tried to love,
but I failed
Now I hold a heart
that has been nailed.
Why won't the crying stop?
It hurts too much to bear
His hand trying to touch me,
it puts me in a deep scare.
I want to die quickly;
there is nothing to live for.
Escape this cruel world
while they beat me until I'm sore.
Why do they insist on hurting me,
leading me through their lies?
I hope someday soon
everyone chokes and dies.
I've tried to use words
to tell them of my pain
But they only look at me
as being permanently insane.

1998

Afraid of Love

Afraid of love
Is there such a thing

Afraid of love
What would it change

Afraid of love
Would life be a bore

Afraid of love
Is there more

Afraid of love
That tingling feeling

Afraid of love
There is no meaning

Afraid of love
Do you want to be

Afraid of love
Could you be

Afraid of love
Or maybe of loving

1999

Understanding

I sit here with my door ajar
Waiting for a sign to come from afar
I look around the corner,
Not knowing what to expect
Maybe someone who will connect
Not looking for anyone particular
Just a hand to touch and a heart to lure
I look to the sky
Wishing I could fly
I step on the ground
And start to wander around
Kids run past me with smiles on their faces
I want to run to so many places
I reach out to touch this thing called life
But it cowards away out of the light
I take a drink of my sweetened tea
Wishing happiness could flow through me
I look at my life as compared to before
Though my past was worse, I want more

1999

My Ignorance to You

Beauty is but a word
Destroyed to your advantage
Quite overly whispered
And usually rapes my image

My body is but a tool
Forced to live for my mind
I wish my body would wake up
And rewind
To be 100 lbs. or so
And pretty, as far as you can see,
Blame my ignorance on society

My personality is nothing to treasure
It's a waste of space in my mind
What do you expect to profit from me
There is nothing here worth your time

I know you really want me
But not for what's in my soul
Instead, for my ignorance, or FORCED body,
To you I bestow.

2002

Holding On To...

Cast iron heart
So cold and protected
Lets no love invade
Loves none and none trusted

Mixed emotions come common
And screaming everyday
Only tears come of this
And no words to say

Does love even linger near you
Any temptation to lust
Is nothing there for me
Has it all been crushed to dust

I have been lost for awhile
But there was eagerness to get it back
Motivation is slowly dying
What once was, is now partly cracked

2005

What's Fair

Why is there mistrust
When all I give is love
Yelling at me comes easy
It's as harsh as a shove
Why not abuse me
Yet, you're already there
Being skeptical is becoming natural
Little items make me aware
Could you love me again
The way you did in the beginning
Or are you exhausted of me
And your love descending
I try my best to do everything for you
With love, honesty, and care
Yet you still treat me different
It all seems too unfair

2005

All I Need

All I need is one smile
To keep me alive
Only need acknowledgment
To stay happy inside

All I need is strength
To stand firm while in pain
Only need comfort
To stand in the rain

All I need is love
To have a reason to fight
Only need encouragement
To stay focused on the light

All I need is one soul
To keep me company while I fall
Only one hand to keep me up
And he's there when I call

2006

Mind or Heart

I can feel it
When you look into my eyes
My heart begins to crush
And I want to lie down and die

Your behavior always changes
You're a different person every day
First I think you love me
Then there's nothing to say

I'm so damn confused
I don't know what to do
Should I runaway
Or stay here with you

My heart believes you're the one
My mind disagrees every night
I don't know if I can have you or not
Which one is right

I keep thinking I need you to live
Like you're the food to my hunger of love
Should I listen to what's beating in my chest
Or should I go with what's being said above

2006

Absolute Love?

I want to feel true love again
The kind of love that makes you laugh
While it makes you cry
So many emotions…you can't think straight

I want someone to look at me
Feel just as giddy and hopeless
Treat me as a princess should be
See me as if I walk on water

Though shy and timid in public
Show me off as if you want the world to know
Feel as if you acquired what everyone wants
Grasp the emotions and ride free

Can you truly say you've met someone like me?
Does the goofiness not excite you?
Does the professionalism not turn you on?
A little girl one moment, a strong woman the next

I don't ask for much
Just to be loved and trusted
To be truthful and honest with me
No matter how much it hurts

(continued)

Can you handle this much?
Trust, love, giddiness, goofiness, a strong independent woman?
Am I too difficult to handle?
Is it like driving with no steering wheel?

I'm afraid
To let down my wall made of strong will
To remain an independent and tough woman
Are you strong enough to tear it down?

Don't let the 'newness' fool you
It tends to blind you to the truth
Makes you believe it is going to be forever
Is it the 'newness' or is it absolute love?

2007

Everything Changes In Time

We were always so playful
Mastering 'donuts' in the snow
Visiting pet stores and shelters to play
While acquiring a 'herd' of animals of our own

Our likes and dislikes seemed to work off each other
While criticizing each other's imperfections
No feelings hurt, just laughter followed
Knowing that the other would never think such things

As time went by, our love grew weak
Trust was not a mutual feeling
Crying was more common than laughing
'Giddiness' and laughter was substituted by sadness and depression

After more time went by and trying to fix things seemed impossible
I felt, in order to save what love we had left, I needed to leave
Becoming easily annoyed and wanting to be elsewhere
Were feelings that were more common than patience and happiness

(continued)

Though not 'in love', my love for you will never end
You still make me smile
I still think of you everyday
And the tears have changed from sadness to missing you

I'd still wear your ring
While it symbolizes the love we had
The fun that almost always took place
And the memories I will never forget

Though I know we will never be together again
I feel that this one symbolic item would treasure our love
And as the tears roll down my face now
Know that you will always be in my heart

Time will mend our hearts
The tears will slowly fade
We will then realize what was done was right
And our love will live on forever

2007

False Hopes

Sometimes the world seems to crash
On top of your shoulders bringing you down
Farther than the earth's surface
Where you drag your feet every day

All seems good and well until that moment
When realization kick drops your gut 'til you fall
As you stare down at the gravel and dirt beneath you
The noise surrounding you seems to take your breath away

It's so loud you can barely hear your ankles and wrists cracking
As you attempt to stand once again
Your thoughts seem so sporadic and unorganized
That trying to decipher them only causes more pain

(continued)

Trying to acknowledge your surroundings
But the glare from all the critics seem to blind you
You shield your eyes but only to realize the noise again
This time, not your own thoughts, but theirs

The tears running down your cheeks are so cool
But you barely notice the wetness when shaking
Lips quivering, throat and chest tightening
As the sadness and frustration dances on your face

You then realize while still gripping the rocks, you never stood up
Feels as though someone splashed your face with warm water
Blood coming from corners of your hands, tears from the corner of your eyes
Once again, sadness took over and standing up was only ever a silly dream

2007

What's Kept Inside

How do you know
You're following the right path
Life changes so often
Choices are constantly made

How do you know
If your heart or mind is speaking
When everything you do
Is not for you
Pleasing everyone
Is what you do

Yea, I'm smiling everyday
Inside I'm dying,
Screaming,
Tears saying what I can't
Holding back
Words I want to scream

Emotions played out
In my head, dropping
Ideas of painful, lethal,
Uncomfortable actions

(continued)

Sometimes,
It takes every ounce
Of the little energy I have
To not surrender
To those thoughts

How do I know
If all will end well
If the grass isn't greener
That it is possible to feel
More than sadness,
Numbness,
And an un-caring mind set

If I surrender,
Can I start over
Would I follow the same paths
Would life and its minions
Throw me around
Like the ragdoll I've always been

Unknown ideas
Will stay just that
As I continue to follow
The same path.

2007

Sick and Tired

Now sick to my stomach
The crying has come back strong
Why is it so hard?
Why do I keep falling apart?
My body is shaking
Goosebumps cover me
I feel weak
Is pushing you away
Making me sick?
I know I love you
I have never doubted that
People always said
You know when it's no longer right
…they were right
I fought to keep us together
Wore myself thin
I soon realized
Nothing will ever change
And loving you
Just wasn't enough

2007

Describing Love

As I lay in bed
The absence of you grows stronger.
Before,
I could barely breathe,
Now,
No air escapes me.
The pain in my chest
Compares to pain felt
When having no food for days.
When I say "I need you",
It's not an elementary form
Of intense love but
The actual necessity of you
Being in my everyday life.
Don't take this sadness as a fault
On one of us but the effects of being torn
From a life necessity,
I am dying without you.
My love for you is eternal.

2008

Lonely...Again

There's that stinging pain again
When I thought it finally left
Casting my insecurities away
Their screams so loud, I feel deaf

I knew better and wonder why I hoped
I try so hard to catch his attention
To be what he wants me to be
My attempts seem lost in translation

Does love ALWAYS have to be this difficult
So full of tears, doubts and pain
I feel like crying and it's so familiar
But my tear ducts are dry again

Maybe loneliness is the only choice for me
At least the shock of it will be expected
No doubts of what he's thinking
Just my insecurities and me, disrespected

2013

THE ARTISTIC HEART

Friends Forever

Come what may too soon life's end
The day I die without a friend
What a miserable death that day would be
When I am welcomed to eternity
The road that lies ahead is rough
But apologizing is not enough
You, my friend, is all it's worth
To live happily on planet Earth
To be with you my life is grand
To say goodbye while holding your hand
This would be life's greatest thrill
To stop all clocks and hold time still
I will be apart from you never
Because we will be friends forever

1998

To You From Me

Here at your job, you work all day
Trying to make a living, trying to get a pay
You wonder why, it hasn't struck five
Hoping it would soon come by
Here is something that may help you,
Right now, I'm thinking of you
I hope you have a good 'ole day
Working your tail off to get that pay
Now to end, I say with this poem
Once you're done, I'll be here and, to me, you can come home

Written for my Mom

1998

Five Haiku

While my fingernails
Rip down your back, a sense of
Connection moves me.

Tears screaming down my
Soft cheek illustrate my pain
Of your missed absence.

Caressing a sheet
Of paper, the pen feels at
Ease, guided by words.

Leaping through the night
Kittens play with each other
Then sleep through the day.

Waiting patiently
For the scared, unknowing mouse-
She pauses, then strikes.

2000

Her Emotions

Trickling down your cheek
Cold drops of hard rain
Harsh sound of thunder
A sad world crying out in pain

Lightning, an understood warning
From earth to human beings
Leave the world at peace
Listen to her feelings

Taste earth's scented flowers
Smell her sweet trees
Gaze at her mountains
Feel her luring breeze

Live as you will
Lay happily in her when you die
Handle with care
Earth's delicate organs of life

2000

Just the Two of Us

From the start you were there
I was the first to explore your care
You raised me to be the best
And blessed me with your chest
In many ways, we're so alike
Complex like Pop's big bike
We read our books
Similar looks
Delicate hands
Strong demands
Our long blonde hair
Makes our men stare
Our life was really rough
But we finally said enough
I feel as if I'm closer to you
Because we were together before them two
You will always be the best mom ever
All the other moms will take your place, never
You know he is good for me too
And that I will always love you
I'll be gone someday
But in my heart you'll stay
If we weren't family, together
I believe we would be friends forever

For My Mom on Mother's Day

2000

Visual Aid

Inspired by Joseph Vogel's "Vision"

An insipid, yet eye-catching "Picasso",
this gray and white distraction
shows a single-handed cat starving, searching
for a cuisine from a scattered
garbage can (not quite full)
tipped over
littering the matter around
her. She hasn't noted
the skinny Rover, tail to the trash
not quite as jaded,
determined to get attention
from this peculiar man
standing alone.
Reading or singing,
with his chin in the air, far out
enough to place a dinner
platter on, arms stretched,
holding onto an object
(book or paper) he isn't looking at. A poor man hanging
from a cross, fears no more
who will hurt him today,
will he eat tomorrow.
Two other articles, distortions of humans,
not aware of what is going on. Bits
and pieces floating above,
in no certain disposition
taking shape in rectangles and squares,
synchronized with the narrator's words. Oblivious
to the visual he resumes, speaking in tones,
with his unknown eyes
shut.

2000

Joseph Vogel's "Vision"

What a Rush

While you glide down my throat
I get this sensation
I'm taking off the edge
Awaiting your creation
All I can think about
As I take in your liquid
Is your cool sweet taste
And I'm so addicted
As I press your mouth to mine
I start to close my eyes
Waiting impatiently for your love
As you go down my slide
Now we're all done
As we sit here in a hush
I take in a deep breath, whispering
Snapple, what a rush

2000

Company

He was born when I was
And he walks when I do
He eats when I eat
And is attached to my shoe.

He follows me to school
Then follows me home
He hides behind a tree
Or hides under a stone.

He comes out with the sun
And hides in the night
He stands where I stand
And fights when I fight.

He goes where I go
He cries when I cry
And someday my shadow
Will die when I die.

2001

There I Was, A Vampire

While you're sucking my blood
I'm licking your wounds
A vampire's glory yet to be abused.

As your teeth go through my neck
You're corrupting my soul
My death has become my birth
Death, now, I do control.

You start to pull away
Still holding onto me
My teeth start to sharpen
And his blood starts to bleed.

As I reach for his neck
A stake goes through my heart.
I screech with pain and blow apart.

2002

Only One

A solitary hand is needed to reach out
Keeping in touch with one forever
Wanting to express your feelings of love and frustration
While acting as the world's care giver

A solitary person is needed
To make a single person feel special
Putting forward an effort towards kindness
When your entire world is becoming unstable

A solitary emotion expressed
Says all too much on how one feels
No words needed to be spoken or shown
What your eyes can and will reveal

You're a solitary woman
With ages of emotions as big as the world
I reach out my hand to you
Holding my love and appreciation in a solitary pearl

Inspired by the woman who always held strong,
Grandma Beverly Christensen 1935 to 2009

2005

STAND UP!

I've been hit hard with criticism
From people who don't take the time
Assumptions are made with ignorance
Going on as if they've caused no crime

Making crude comments
About my size or the way I dress
Why I do my job when I'm supposed to
And how I couldn't be worth any less

These people are full of emptiness
Feeding off one's weaknesses at will
With no values or cares in their world
No concern of whose self-worth they kill

Every day, after everything is said and done
You feel as if you want to lie down and die
Make those people happy with your absence
Just give in and stop asking 'Why?'

I'm done giving in to their immaturity
Done with their comments and glares
Finished with their consistent pettiness
I'm standing up and fighting for what's fair

2006

Love Him

Love comes unexpected
When the world seems it's coldest
Always unsure to take that chance
Feeling vulnerable, not the boldest

When it's the right love
What you do or believe doesn't matter
Your life now seems to make sense
Religion, friends and family; no longer factors

You can't help who you love
You can't change people's minds
You can't reason with your feelings
But with love, you can stop time

Love him as you would no other
Support him when others don't
Believe in him when your own opinions may differ
And always cherish him when others won't

My Best "Man" speech for my best friend Dan Cannon & his husband,
Doug Meissel's, wedding. I will love you forever.

2012

THE INTOXICATED HEART

Claustrophobic

I can feel it
Feel it coming
It's impossible
Stop spinning
Your mind starts dancing
You start moving
You can't get out
It's so confusing
You feel sick to your stomach
Things start getting blurry
Your mind goes wild
And you begin to scurry
Everyone notices you now
Your fear is mounted
You think it's you
But it's just crowded

1996

Communicating

I hear voices
In my head
I hear them
When I'm going to bed
I try to ignore them
As they chatter away
They must be crazy
If they think they're going to stay
They are so incessant
And maybe one day
I'll take leave of my senses
And do what they say
When they go hungry
My brain they ate
Maybe someday
We'll communicate

1997

Thanks to You

Thanks to you
I don't know my name
You're out of my life
And I'm the one to blame

Thanks to you
My mind is cracked
I'm high as a kite
My dreams are black

Thanks to you
I have nothing to do
I scream every night
My life is through

Thanks to you
My candle is burning
My bed is made
My stomach is turning

1997

Vice Versa

I wanted to leave, but I couldn't
I need to stay, yet I shouldn't
You mess with my mind, you will tremble
You look at my face, you will crumble
My fear is my destiny, my love is my fate
My looks could kill, but it's too late
You did control me, but now I control you
This poem is finished, and you are through.

1997

Dazed and Confused

You're laughing out loud
Yet no one hears you
You're feeling great
But about to spew

You cried all night
Yet didn't shed a tear
Not scared of anything
But you feel the fear

You're about to die
Yet in the greatest mood
You think you're eating a pear
But it's really a prune

You're talking to someone
Yet your mouth hasn't moved
You think you got a raise
But you woke up and you're screwed.

1998

He Came Back

I made friends with a dead man
I was so scared, I ran
The fear within me
Made it hard to breathe
I stopped for breath
And instead smelled death
I started to scream
But a dead hand caught me
The smell of death became stronger
As my mind started to wonder
How did I get in this situation?
Then I felt all the tension
It's hard to believe
This dead man is holding me
He turned me around
I fell in love at what I found
Now I'm stuck in darkness
In love with this man
How strange this all ends
Believe it, if you can.

1999

Reality Check

You think you know me
But find out I'm truly bad
Like a girl who looks happy
When inside, she's sad.

I try to please the best I can
But can't conquer all things
Never got sweet roses
Or fine diamond rings.

I won't answer to anyone
Until I feel I'm ready to
I'm going to have my fun
Doing what I want to do.

Since you've read this poem
I'll give you a little peck!
Ha! In your dreams!
Reality Check.

1999

Driving

As I make a turn
And look
The other way, I notice
Half
The time I'm driving
I don't pay attention.

Driving for minutes at
A time, I realize I've
Been spacing.

Staring at my "dash",
I wonder many things
About what is not
Going on around
Me, yet I seem to make it
To my destination.

(continued)

I use my turn
Signals and stop
At red lights. I will go
With green and turn
When needed. I am not
Aware of what is around
Me.

I know how to
Drive like I know the back
Of my hand. I can scratch
My second knuckle without
Looking, just like I can drive
Without paying
Attention...

Yet one day I know I will hurt
When I have an incident like
Finding a bruise on the back
Of my hand, not knowing
It was there or how
I got it.

2000

Sweet Dreams

Lying half naked on a pedestal
It's getting kinda cold, but I'm still cool.
People watching me say that I'm a freak
But that's ok because they're meek.
I close my eyes and breathe in the air
I grab a flower and place it in my hair.
I smile at the sun, I wave to the trees
Dance with the beach and swim with the seas.
I watch the birds as I watch the sky
I watch the wind and trees entwine.
Nature is sweet, the environment is clean
I do all these things in my own dreams.
I listen to the sounds that the tigers make
I hear a conversation between two lakes.
They smile as they wink at me
Great love between me and my dreams.
Maybe one day the world will look new
Another day all men will be true.
All these things you will never see
They're locked away in my sweet dreams.

2000

Things

Paper, pens, phones, cups
Beds, tape, kittens, pups
Table, blanket, radio, wall
Jacket, sweater, room, hall
Rainbows, lizards, bags, phones
Book, cat, dog, cones
Picture, poster, box, door
Wait, not quite finished, there's more.

Plug, light, desk, chair
Shirt, shorts, pants, hair
Pet, hanger, shoes, tools
Kitchen, rug, floor, pools
Cord, string, hat, pill
Pillow, boy, girl, mill
Band-Aid, glitter, ferret, polish
Oh, no! I can't embellish.

Glasses, finger, butt, eagle
Cards, colors, Siamese, beagle
Spoons, forks, knives, plate
Poo, I better stop, it's getting late

2000

Senses

I wanna hear
Your ribs crack
While I suck air out of your lungs
As you snap
I wanna see
Your body cringe
As I pull your soul out through your mouth
Like a fringe
I wanna touch
Your skull
As I smash it with my fist
Because you're so dull
I wanna smell your death
Wafting in my nose
As your rotting corpse
Disintegrates in a pose
I wanna taste your blood
Suck it through a straw from your open wound
Filled with maggots that crawl

2002

Dreams Blown in the Wind

You dream of someone
That you'd love to marry
Yet in some strange way
You seem wary
Then you dream of luxury
And your real life is faded
But then you realize
It all seems painted
Now you dream of you
You're perfect in every way
But when you take a second glance
Your face starts to decay
After all this
They come to an end
And you noticed your dreams
Got blown in the wind

2005

Possibilities

A stranger is a friend
You've never met
A life is a problem
Caught in a net
A book is a world
That has been revived
A father is a king
With a lot of pride
A candle is life
Melting away
A friend is an angel
Watching you pray
A family is an atmosphere
That starts our lives
A mother is a spark
That twinkles in your eyes

2005

THE ENAMORED HEART

Blue Skies

It rained all night,
My sky was gray,
My dreams were nightmares,
Life seemed far away.

My teary eyes never stopped,
I thought it was the end,
Then who would sit beside me,
A good caring friend.

I told him all my troubles,
As he offered me his love,
I thought he was joking,
Until he pointed above.

As I lifted my gaze,
He kissed my face,
My sky was blue again,
And my dreams were in place.

1995

All About You

With you
That's the way it should be

Hug you
Just you and me

Ask you
There's things to tell

Want you
We go so well

Kiss you
So sweet and smoothly

Hold you
Just hold me tightly

Could you
Stay by my side

Would you
Always be mine

Watch you
While you sleep

Miss you
Through the week

Touch you
To hold your hand

I love you

1998

Anticipation

The frustration lingers so close
Every time I think of…
With every wakening glimpse
Illusions teasing my lust

I wonder what would happen
I wonder what…would do
If I let out my sensations
And "play" until I'm blue

The things I can anxiously do
Sensuality at its best
What if I…
Pressure against my chest

Pressing firmly as I …
Yet gentle with my touch
My tongue runs freely
While I …I've said too much

Teasing every luscious inch
Without leading to my best
Will someone play along
Or turn away from my soft awaiting…

1998

Keeping Your Heart

Before I noticed you
You gave me your attention
Then I glanced at you
And felt the strong attraction
I led you away from her
And gave you most of what I got
I loved you through it all
But you loved her as I fought
I'm always going to need you
And want you for all times
I'll never stop loving you
And never forget our crimes
Since you want to be with her
And you have since the start
I'm giving you back
But I'm keeping your heart

1998

My Love

I love the feeling
Of the glistening moonlight
As it dances in the sky all through the night
But when the sun comes out
And it shines on my face
I've forgotten about the moon
And the night has been erased
Our love is like the sun
You're hot and I shine when you're here
But when you leave me all alone
The moon's glisten is in my tears
Then I think of you
And all is perfectly good
My love for you darling
Is in your arms, where I stood

1998

Promises

Every chance that I get
I want to be close to you
I want to hear your perfect lips
Whisper I love you
I think of you every day
And I'm happy we're together
I'm hoping someday
You'll want me to be with you forever
Your kiss melts me
But your hug keeps me from falling
Your smile reassures me
I hear true love calling
Keep me company
To self be true
And through your decisions
I'll be right beside you

1998

The Feel of Love

Do you ever get a sick feeling
Whenever you're around a guy
The kind of feeling
Where you can cough up a fly
Then when he gets closer
There's that tingling sensation
You have an idea
To make a 'you and him' creation
You get closer
To smell his strong cologne
He glances at you
As he gave you a little shove
Then you say to yourself
I've experienced the feeling of love

1998

Delicate Love

The sun curls
my lips into a smile
You put your arms around
me and hug me for awhile
The feel of your fingers on my sides
makes me giggle
The thought of never feeling it again
makes me tremble
I feel your trust in me
when you tell me your secrets
With the advice we give each other,
We're hypocrites
We have minor wounds
in our relationship
But I'm sure our love can mend them
in one trip
I love each and every tender-sweet kiss
From my neck up to my soft-awaiting lips
The gentle touch of your hand
gives me pleasure
And your strength in our love
I will always treasure
When I look in your eyes
I see us getting better
And we'll stay in each other's arms
together forever and ever
My delicate skin awaits you
and I shall "pray"
To feel your touch
Forever, a month, a week and a day.

1999

Falling

I have this sense I'm falling
And I won't hit the ground
I've felt this way for a while
But I haven't made a sound
I notice sometimes I cry
Wet tears of happiness
The farther I fall
The more pressure on my chest
Each day I fall farther
Deeper in the hole
Why am I falling
I would love to know
I always hear a deep voice
Calling out my name
Telling me it loves me
And I say the same
Each time that's said
I get closer to hitting
I fall a little deeper
But it all seems fitting
I have this sense
I want to keep falling
Hit bottom, I don't
But forever hear the calling

1999

My Love to You

I'm crying every night
With my tears in the sea
Hoping some day
You'll truly love me
When you say I love you
And I whisper it back
Those three words
Place us intact
And when you make promises
You better mean every word
If you were to leave me
My heart would rupture
I'll love you with all I have
And give you what you need
I just ask for one thing
For you to always love me

1999

Sssshhhh

Love is precious to whisper
When caring is in the air
Your soft touch feels like a whisker
Delicate on my skin so fair
I look around and begin to wonder
Then drift into a stare
My confused mind starts to ponder
And my dream starts to flair
I see you off near yonder
Where my love will soon be bare
Then I hear that sweet familiar whisper
Teasing my small yearning ear
I wake up to your wanted presence
'I love you' is what I hear

1999

Always Yours

Driving for hours
Having no clue
While you watch the road
I'm adoring you
Watching you sing
Hearing your mature voice
I try to be anorexic
With you, no eating is not a choice
You continuously make me giggle
With your Felipe impression
I am definitely peachy
You give me satisfaction
The way you obsess my eyes
Your gentle touch on my delicate face
Makes me melt in your arms
Where I am put in my place
Your determination with sharing your money
And my stubborn way of refusing it
Brings us closer than ever
Our relationship is full of amusement
I will always love holding onto you
As we walk around the mall
You will always be my baby
And I will always be your baby doll

2002

Sacrifices

You were my bright sunshine
But now you're my fresh air
You have the power to control me
Now tell me what's fair
You wake up with your arms around me
You kiss my morning breath
You'd sacrifice your assets for me
This love will last beyond our death
Sometimes I cry while you're at work
My agony and pain of missing you
You're the best thing that's happened to me
So I promise I will be true
A screaming wet tear
Running down my face
Is what your absence does to me
You never believe a word I say
But still to my heart, I gave you the key
I will always prove you wrong
And we will forever be stubborn
It's a groovy kind of love
Yet a love that will always burn

2002

Wherever You Are

Wherever you are
I'm thinking of you
Wishing you were here
What can I do
Sometimes I cry
Staring at the lamp
I should be with you in a car
Tracing our life on a map
I get lost in your eyes
Wherever you are
You could be next to me
Or dreaming on a star
Sleeping in your arms
So Close and cozy I can hear you snoring
But it doesn't faze me
Wherever you are
My imagination wonders
Is it possible
For this perfect love to last
I will try to make you happy
We will have a blast
I'll always believe you
Thousands wouldn't, but I do
Wherever you are, I'll always love you

2002

Missing You

Come Home!
That's all I can think
I clean house, I work
I only think 'Come Home!'
It seems like eternity since we've kissed
Those foreign lips of lust
Whispering Greek nothings
My heart is racing
Come Home!
Do I need to say it a different way
Does my voice not tell you 'I miss you!'?
Do I need to scream my agony?
Please Moro, come home to me
Walking in a grocery store
Uncrustables…I think of you
In Hobby Lobby, everything is you
I pass by your house
Wanting to run in and lay on your bed
Roll around under the covers until I smell of you
And wait for you to finally come home
Moro Mou…am I saying this out loud?
Seems the rush I feel I can't hide
Seems the wall I built is crumbling
Don't think…just feel hopeless and lost with me
Let's go where our hearts want to go
Love Me…Come Home.

2007

Yes Please

(Two seconds)
Is all I hear in my head
As I look around the corners to see if he's coming.
(I just need two seconds)
As my heart pounds so loud
I can barely hear the guy next to me talking.
(Gawd I'm stupid....)
While trying to calm my nerves
As they race through my body
In anticipation of his smile.
Gawd, that smile that makes me melt like sweet caramel
I feel my face flush and I start to feel really hot
Can this guy tell I've got my mind someplace else?
Nah, he's too enthralled in whatever he's talking about
While clearly staring at my breasts...yes, they're nice.
...Still nothing.
(GAWD, what the hell takes him so long)
I feel as if my heart is about to jump out of my throat.
...Run around the fuckin' corner and ravage his every muscle...

(continued)

(STOP IT), I sound like a horny little school girl (but still, oh my!)
(Shit....) He finally shows, 2 seconds before he needs to be in class
...but that's all I needed.
As he smoothly glides past me with that "fuck me" look in his eyes
(Yes please)
...all I can think is, (damn, what this boy is doing to me is unreal)
He makes it into class just as I realize
The guy next to me is staring at me blankly
"Giggle, Giggle"
...that's all I got.
(Fuck me...)
If only the words and actions that run around my head and tendons
Could speak, or scream...
All I see are walls, tables, his body and mine all coming together
...Pun intended
Still, holding back what may be bliss
Yet awaiting his painfully soft touch and sweet kiss.

2007

Growing Stronger

Our love grows stronger
With every tear we shed
Though the pain we feel now
Makes us feel far, far away instead

As my chest tightens
My pen, alone, begins to empathize
Cause my love for you
Is greater than love, greater in size

My love grows like a flower
And your love is its water and sun
The pains and frustrations we feel now
Will become our future smiles and fun

Our love is beyond comparison
To anything anyone has felt
Your love grows through me
While making my heart and soul melt

I see now in my future
Your hands are guiding me
To love and trust again
To feel true love freely

So when I say those words
That grab your heart and squeeze
Know from the bottom of mine
You'll now only hear 'yes, please'

2008

I Feel You

Tender kisses
From late night to early morning
Gentle touches
Without remorse, without warning

Wrapping together our bodies
Tangling two to become one
Taking in the warmth
As hot as a Cyprus summer sun

Brushing our fingertips
On the contours of each other's faces
Wandering into a timeless bottle
Floating to fantasy and faraway places

Our eyes say the words
While our lips feel each one
Sensations taken for granted
Now we yearn for a closer love

I feel your gentle touch
I feel your warm skin
I feel your loving kisses
On my back, my head, my lips

With my eyes closed
And my heart wide open
You heal every inch of me
Everything that has ever been broken

2008

It's Just Me and You

The world could end tomorrow
And I will still choose to stay in your arms
While the world crashes around us
I will see nothing but you

No matter the troubles that find us
New hurdles to jump over
We will handle it all together
And prove the impossible to be possible

Don't let silly things like money, boundaries or family
Distract you from where we are going
Our love will keep us together, stronger than ever
And our love will surpass any obstacle thrown at it

I can't tell you exactly how I feel now, it's so complicated…
It's mixtures of love, frustrations, goals, compromises
And most of all…determination
To prove to the world, it can't tear us apart

We got this…
This and everything else we want to accomplish together
As long as we have each other, the world will never win
It's you and me against the world baby…and it's just the beginning!

2008

My [Disintegrating] Wall

Summer curiosities
Bloom into winter love
Though the world is frozen now
White roses blossom in my eyes with thoughts of you

Weightless and indescribably happy
I feel as if I'm a wingless angel
Here only to be your muse
To entertain going further

I'm not ready to fall in love
But love is ready for me
It tugs and whispers to my shattered heart
Whispering sweet promises, romantic waves of lust
While caressing my dreams with yours
Turning expected empty promises into forgotten thoughts

You cared enough to break down my wall,
My crumbled doubts and insecurities, piece by piece
With a warm confident smile,
A smile that could make any strong woman weak with desire

I take this path day by day with hopes
That I will be in your arms again
While our heartbeats harmonize
And our insecurities disappear.

2008

To Be or Not To Be?

When you're near me
I feel as if
I'm six miles from the sun
The way you make my blood boil
How my heart blisters from your rays

As my toes curl under your legs
I feel your gaze
On my every part
Always watching me, analyzing
When did you start loving me?

I think,
I'm so tired of December,
Winter is boring me
I'm ready for a new season
One filled with happiness,
Fun and excitement
One without the stresses of life
Pushing me down

I refocus
As I attempt to gaze back
At your tempting eyes
I become filled with joy and laughter
I stop
And lay my head on your knee
...I want to be your beautiful disaster

2008

Truly, Madly, Deeply Yours

As I listen to the soundtrack of our love,
I picture us holding each other in darkness.
No words are spoken.
We just breathe.

Why is it that we are so happy but we cry?
Is love not treating us right?
OR…is our love so strong that it breaks the boundaries of emotions,

Releasing the ever-so-needed, bounded-by-pain, mystery of passion?
We are so strong, even when it hurts.

Accomplishing a fixation for real 'true love' and 'happy endings',
Sometimes lost and blinded by love, we
Disregard previous connections with past loves.

I want to do meaningless things with you forever.
Stroll in the rain
When dressed for another occasion.
Lie in the grass and determine
What the stars are trying to show us.
Dance to static on an AM radio.

Love treats everyone different and leads us in different paths
It makes us believe, or not believe,
What others see or don't see.
Whatever this may be that we are experiencing together…
…this is what I pictured 'in love' to be.
Truly, Madly, Deeply Yours.

2008